Why Darkness Seems So Light:

Young People Speak Out about Violence

Helen Frost, editor

Pecan Grove Press
Box AL
1 Camino Santa Maria
San Antonio, Texas 78228-8608

Copyright © 1998

by Helen Frost

Drawing on page 13 by Justin J. Jordan
Cover and all other art by Theoplis Smith

This project was initiated by the Fort Wayne YWCA as part of their annual Week Without Violence awareness campaign, and by Harvey Cocks of the Fort Wayne Youtheatre.

ISBN: 1-877603-58-9

Pecan Grove Press
Box AL
1 Camino Santa Maria
San Antonio, Texas 78228-8608

Acknowledgements

A project such as this one requires the input and support of many people.

I thank the Fort Wayne YWCA, especially Priscilla Greene, Becky Hill, Carla Nunez, Kris Richey and Judy Thomas, for initiating this project, as part of their annual Week Without Violence awareness campaign, and for doing the planning and fund raising for it. Financial support has come from several local businesses including Target, NBD, Tokheim, and Don R. Fruchey, Inc.

Thanks to Harvey Cocks, of the Fort Wayne Youtheatre, for co-authoring and directing a play based on students' writing. Throughout the project, Harvey has been a source of support in many ways.

I thank all the teachers and principals who invited me to their schools (Alternative Learning Program, Heritage, Homestead, North Side, South Side, and Wayne High Schools). Special thanks to teachers Susan Boesch, Ellen Figel, Cindy Kennell, Barbara Lawrence, Jennifer Peckham, Stephanie Pickett, Scott Sowers, Lynn Stoller, Jerry Vohs, and Lynn Yoder.

"Death in His Eyes," by Danielle Hillworth, first appeared in *The Journal Gazette*, May 17, 1998, and is reprinted here with permission.

All the stories are included with the permission of the authors, and where the author is under the age of eighteen, with the permission of a parent or guardian.

Many students contributed their writing, and we could not use all of their stories in this book, but without their cooperation and hard work, the book would not have been possible. I thank them, and the parents who encouraged them.

Thanks to Thomas A. Herr, attorney, for his careful reading of the manuscript with an eye for legal concerns.

Palmer Hall, of Pecan Grove Press, had the vision to see a potential book in the early drafts of the manuscript. Thank you, Palmer, for seeing it through.

And I thank my husband, Chad Thompson, and my sons, Lloyd and Glen, for their interest and understanding.

Dedicated to
those who should be present,
who have been taken from us
too soon.

Table of Contents

. . .if we let it hurt us, it's hard to live, it's hard to survive

. . .I began to feel a pain I never wanted to feel

. . .I can't live in one terrible moment the rest of my life.

Why Darkness Seems So Light
Introduction

In the spring of 1998 in Fort Wayne, Indiana, I went into six public high schools—urban, rural, and suburban—and asked students to write stories in response to the question, "Have you ever been personally affected by violence?" Only about ten students said, no, they had no experience of violence, and only a few others declined to write about their experience. 249 students wrote something. The stories included in this book represent the range of experience and emotion they shared. From witnessing a boy being struck by his father in a parking lot, to bearing responsibility for the death of a friend, or coming to terms with the murder of a parent or the suicide of a sibling—these stories show how profoundly the young people in one community have been affected by the violence that has become so pervasive in our country.

The title "Why Darkness Seems so Light," raises the question that many young people and adults are trying to answer. We can see, as we read the newspaper and look around us, that violence is not uncommon. But how have so many people become so casual about it? Another case of domestic violence, another drug-related shooting, another fight in the school hallways. If darkness is all around us, these stories suggest, it begins to seem light, in both senses. We cease to recognize it as darkness, and we become unaware of its weight on our shoulders.

It is my hope in editing this book, that by looking straight at this darkness, we will come to recognize it for what it is. That may be the first step in making it lighter.

In the handwritten copy of Chelsea Cella's story, she first wrote "Why Darkness Is So Light." She crossed out "is" and wrote "seems"—in that simple change I saw the human mind at work, the struggle to tell the truth. There were many instances of such struggles. One student wrote

"I do not forgive him," crossed out "not," then wrote it in again, and scrawled "Not Finished" across the bottom of the paper. Another student wrote that he and his father did not speak to each other for two weeks, then amended it to say that, while he did not speak to his father for two weeks, every night before he went to bed, his father said, "I'm sorry." Forgiveness, compassion, loyalty, honesty about self and others—these are some of the things I admire in these stories. Many of the stories are difficult to read, but in most cases, along with the troubling elements of brutality, there is something redeeming, or some reach towards understanding.

I have organized the stories in sections, roughly defining different kinds of involvement with violence. The stories in the first section deal with childhood memories, followed by a group of stories about more recent things that have happened, then stories of personal involvement in violence. This is followed by a section about why it is often hard to feel emotion, even in the face of trauma, and in the next section, the writers describe times when they have felt strong emotion. The final group of stories makes a strong start at coming to terms with the violence the writers describe.

As editor, I have made some small changes for the sake of clarity, brevity, or privacy. I've edited out language that might offend some readers, unless it is essential to the story, and I've deleted most references to race and ethnic background. A number of people have asked me about that, and I would just like to say that the stories in this book come from people of all backgrounds, in much the same proportions as the population of the community. Although poverty may cause some of the frustrations out of which violence can arise, wealth does not seem to offer much shelter.

When the students were writing, I wanted them to feel safe, and I told them that they could write anonymously or fictionally. Please do not assume that all the factual details of these stories are accurate, as many changes have been made in order to protect the writers and the people in their stories. Still, when I selected stories for the book, one of the things I looked for was an authentic voice. Whether or not the facts have been altered, I think the stories carry an essential truth.

This truth is not just about Fort Wayne, Indiana. There may be some who question the wisdom of publicly portraying such a negative side of an otherwise vital and caring community. For similar reasons, many of the students were reluctant to tell stories about their friends and families, yet when they listened to each other's stories, they often found relief in knowing that others had been through similar experiences. When this book is read in other communities, it may serve a similar purpose. I hope the stories we have told here will open a discussion, both in Fort Wayne, and in other cities and towns where violence is a problem, and that the discussion will help to turn us towards greater peace.

This is not a book to read from cover to cover in one sitting. Absorbing the pain of many of these stories takes time and emotional energy. Once, after a particularly difficult week, listening to and reading some of the hardest stories, a young man in one of the classes asked me, "How can you keep doing this without getting depressed?" It was a good question, and, in a way, it was its own answer. The work seems to generate the kind of compassion his question embodied, not just for me, but for each other, and for strangers.

It is my hope that such compassion may allow readers to appreciate, too, the loveliness of some of the quiet moments: a cat climbing into the lap of a distraught young girl, a boy deciding not to run away, a mother giving her last stick of butter to a hungry child. And that father, every night for two weeks, saying to his son "I'm sorry."

We have a lot to learn from these young voices. Listen.

Helen Frost
1998

...the faint cry from the baby upstairs

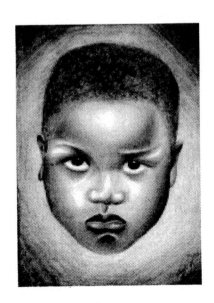

Crisula Arapios

Faint Cry

It is a nice day. She comes in the door and sits down in the blue chair that is close to the big wooden door.

Sitting there watching T.V. with the faint cry from the baby upstairs. She sits there and the 3-year-old on her left. And the irritating smell from the cigarette that is pressed against her lips.

Then the sound of the mailbox and the door opens. The big dark shadow comes over her. Then the angry voice and the sound of the slap against her skin.

The little voice screams STOP! STOP IT! and another slap against skin and then the silence.

Then the sound of the slamming door and the heavy footsteps leave the house.

She sits there wondering, when will it be over? When will it all stop? And then the small cry from upstairs and at the same time the phone rings.

"It is nice to hear a familiar voice," she says to the other voice on the other end of the line.

Carmen Warner

Cubby Hole Partner

It was almost time for the bell to ring in Mrs. Moore's first grade class, the last day before spring break. We put our worksheets in the cubby, June's on top of mine.

We were always partners, being the two smallest girls in class. She was quiet and sweet, her pants always grass-stained, hair nappy and unbrushed; me, loud and happy, never seen without a grin. We were an odd couple, maybe that's why we were perfect together.

Walking down the sidewalk on that damp, spring day, I babbled on and gossiped while June quietly listened and occasionally chuckled. We came to the big tree, and I grinned and said goodbye. As she turned the corner, she looked back and I could see the corners of her mouth turn upward a bit. If I had known that was going to be the last time I saw her, I would have tried harder to make her smile like I usually did.

I walked home and got my milk and cookies. June stopped at a friend's house, then cut through an alley on her way home.

There were so many different rumors and stories about what happened next. I'm just going to say what I remember of them.

She was walking down the alley when some men jumped out and grabbed her, dragging her to their car—stealing her from her family, her home, and her cubby hole partner.

She must have struggled, considering all the bruises and bumps that she had. I guess beating her must have bored them, so they decided to take her innocence, one by one violating her in the utmost disgusting way, killing her, little by little, piece by piece.

Their fun must have been finished when they decided to dump her off. It wasn't until a few days later that the people who were searching for her found her in some woods, lifeless and cold, raped, bruised, broken and bleeding. The many stab wounds were obvious as she lay there dead for days in the bushes.

Why didn't she go home and get her milk and cookies? Why did I get mine?

I missed my cubby hole partner. No longer did she put her worksheet on top of mine. First grade did end, but I'll never forget our parting that day. Our parting forever.

Kyla Thompson

Scared

It was summertime and I decided to visit my cousin in Detroit. My cousin and I were both the same age, about 11.

Her mom let us go to the park one afternoon while she went to Bible study. So my cousin Amber, my other cousin Robbie (age 10), Amber's friend Breanna and I hopped in the car so we could leave.

"Stay together and don't run off," said my aunt as we all got out of the car. "I'll be back in about an hour," she yelled, and she drove off.

We all ran off to the swings and began to play. We played for about 20 minutes until two boys came walking towards us. They were both about 13 years old and they were shaped like teenage boys and had a little muscle on them.

I hopped off the swing and walked over to talk to my cousin. Robbie and Breanna were still on the swings. The two boys had said something about Robbie, so then he made a smart kind of kiddish remark to them. The two boys kept on saying things and talking.

Then Breanna said, "Why don't you two shut up and leave him alone?"

I looked at Breanna, then turned and looked at Amber. "Do you know them, Amber?" I said quietly.

"Nope," she responded.

One of the boys had a broken arm and he had a white cast on it. He looked at Breanna angrily and said, "Don't talk to my uncle like that." Now this may confuse you, but yes, the two boys were uncle and nephew, both 13.

So Breanna got off of her swing and stood there and looked him straight in the face and said, "I'll talk to your uncle however I want to."

Then unexpectedly one of the boys just jumped on her and started punching her. Then the other, with the broken arm, began kicking her on her back and in her stomach.

My cousin Amber and I were just standing there, fearful and not knowing what to do. The park was empty and there was no one to run to. Robbie was still swinging on the swing.

They still kicked and punched Breanna. Then finally they stopped and walked away.

Breanna lay in the sand, clothes dusty and filthy, crying, "Why didn't you help me?"

I was scared. That was my first time ever in my life seeing someone getting beat up right in front of my face.

We pulled her up off the ground, still crying. Then Amber's mom pulled up. She stepped out of the car and yelled at all of us, "What's going on? What happened? Why is Breanna crying?"

We all just stood there with a dumbfounded look upon our faces. Then finally Amber said, "Breanna just got jumped by two boys."

"Did you all help her? Why didn't you help her?" she yelled at us furiously.

We piled in the car. Breanna sat in the front still whimpering and silently crying. Nobody said anything. It was a silent ride home.

When we finally pulled up to the driveway, my aunt said to us in a powerful soft tone of voice, "Get out of the car, and when you all get in the house, sit down on the couch. Don't get up for anything."

The rest of the night my aunt gave us a little lecture about how we should have helped Breanna and that even though the two boys were older, there were more of us and just two of them.

When I was younger, I was still scared, and I just thought of it as there was nothing we could do. Now when I think about what happened, I realize I actually could have helped Breanna by just telling her to ignore what the boys were saying.

Edna Ruth Hepworth

The Murder of Angela

Here is my story. My Dad was a drunk. He used to hit me all the time. He would hit me until I got tired. My mom died when I was a little girl. She had a heart attack when I was 6.

It all started on a cold winter morning. I lived with my Aunt Angela. She was a beautiful nice lady, 37 years old. She had a husband named Edward and a daughter named Sherrell. We all lived in a house. It wasn't a real big house, but she always took care of us. She made sure we were fed and had clothes on our backs.

My aunt got up late and she was cooking me some breakfast. Edward came into the house after being drunk. Angela told me to go into the other room. I only stayed in the room for a minute. Edward was hitting Angela. I did not like seeing her getting hit because I know what it feels like to be hit and to be hurt.

Edward grabbed a knife out of the drawer and he stabbed her 38 times in the back. I got scared and went into a corner and curled up in a ball and cried. Sherrell called 911. When the ambulance came, Angela was dead. She lost so much blood.

I lost my family again. I kept asking Sherrell, "Where is Angela?" Sherrell told me that Angela wouldn't be coming back.

Edward will be in jail for three more years. I've seen him and he says he's changed and when he gets out he wants to see me.

How come he had to take a human life? What happened on that cold winter morning should never have happened.

Cravana Brew

My Friend's Secret

When I was younger, I had this friend. We had been good friends from about second grade to fifth grade. She always seemed like the average normal little girl. She smiled a lot and was rarely in a bad mood. Little did I know she had problems, or more like one big problem.

I was spending the night at her house one night, and that's when she told me. I was in fifth grade, barely old enough to understand what she was to tell me. We were in her room talking and she started telling me how she had been molested by her uncle for the past six years.

I was shocked! What can you say when someone tells you something like that? So I just sat there and listened to her as she told me everything that he had done to her. She told me how sometimes he would threaten her and sometimes he would bribe her with gifts or tell her that she was so beautiful. She told me how she had felt trapped and helpless her whole life.

I wondered why she hadn't told me sooner (now her parents and some relatives knew). She didn't tell me until it was all over. I didn't want to ask her though, because I didn't want to put her on the spot. I knew it was very hard for her. All she needed right now was a friend to stand by her and help her through this, not someone who was going to keep asking questions or criticize her. I'm not sure what I said to her, if anything at all. But I think I was of help to her.

She ended up suing him. She sued him for everything he had, and won. She gave it all back to his wife though. She didn't want any of his money, it was just the principle of it. And she didn't think his wife should suffer for what he did.

I haven't really talked to her since the sixth grade. We both moved on to different schools and kind of grew apart. As far as I know, everything turned out all right.

Jared Frieden

Summer of '93

In the summer of '93 my friends and I decided to build a fort in the woods near my house. So Sam stayed the night at my house, and we got up at the crack of dawn and met up with Ryan and Zack at Zack's house. We walked through the woods for several hours until we finally found a great place to build a fort.

The leaves were so thick and green, they provided plenty of cover. The tree was nice and big, perfect for our ideas. The branches at the top almost formed a platform. We worked on it for many days, scaring away every animal that was remotely close to us, with the echoes from the hammer and all our laughing.

We worked really hard and built our best. We even had booby traps set up around the base of the tree. When we were finished we had a nice place to hang out and talk to our friends.

It was a very peaceful place. I could sit up there for hours and listen to the birds singing, squirrels running, and the noise from the nearby road. We even had a lookout which let us see almost anything. We had planned a quick way to exit in case of an emergency; we had our swing to add to the fun.

But one day everything seemed strange. There was a chilly breeze, and some dark clouds in the sky. The birds weren't singing as loud as usual. As we were sitting up in the fort we heard some branches cracking.

Sam went to the lookout and saw three boys coming near. Sam shouted down from the high lookout to warn us of what was near. We all got in our positions and waited quietly. The boys heard us talking and shot a rock at us with their slingshot.

Of course we were always prepared so we grabbed our slingshots and rocks. We fought to protect our fort like in the old days with cowboys and Indians.

We finally drove them off and none of us were hit. I wasn't sure about them. We thought everything was cool, so we went home for the evening.

The next day when we met up again, we walked back to the fort, but that same eerie feeling was there. When we got to the point where we could see our fort, we noticed something different. We got closer and noticed that our cover was all cut down; the limbs were laying on the ground, the leaves all shriveled. The fort itself wasn't bad—we had built it tough.

We fixed what we could and let nature do its thing. Eventually the trees grew back, the leaves got green, and everything was the way we had liked it. We spent many fun days there. Now I am too busy to go back there, with work and all. Or maybe I just outgrew it.

Rachel Jackson

Children Come First: Don't Turn Away

Setting:
House, all the furniture in the living room. Sound of a saw.

Characters:
Mom (Terry): Long grey scraggly hair, short and chunky, glasses with tape on them because they're broken.
Dad (Ralph): Tall, but hunched over. Black curly hair. Dirty pants on, with knee pads.
Sister (Sara): (age 12) Tall, skinny. Long brown hair.
Sister (Rachel): (age 14) Long dark hair pulled in pony tail.
Little Girl: (about 5 or 6) Wearing old clothes and a coat that's too small for her.

Script:
Mom: *Ralph, we need to get this room done. Come on.*
Ralph: *OK. I have to take my time. You can't rush putting a floor down.*
          (knock at the door)
Sara: *Who's here?*
Rachel: *I don't know. Maybe Mary.*
Sara: *Mom, someone's here—a little girl asking for food or money.*
Terry (goes to the door): *Can I help you?*
Little girl: *Do you have any food or money for me and my little sisters and brothers?*
Terry: *I only have 2 dollars. I just gave the rest to my daughter. Come in the kitchen.*
Ralph: *What do you need? Where's your mom and dad?*
Little Girl: *I don't live with my dad. My mom's at home.*
Rachel: (entering room) *Where do you live?*
Little Girl: *Two houses down, on that street.*

Rachel: *Mom, I need to get some hot curlers so I can go out.*
Little Girl: *You're going out tonight?*
Rachel: *Yeah, to Lazer-X.*

(Terry is getting a little food that most people would take for granted, and putting it in a bag.)
Terry: *Rachel, see if there's a stick of butter in the fridge.*
Rachel: *No, I don't see any. Oh, here is is. It's the last one.*
Terry: *Give it to me anyway.*
Little Girl: *That should fill us up at least 'til tomorrow.*
(Terry and the little girl walk into the other room.)
Terry: *Where's that candy that was here?*
Rachel: *It's over there.*
Terry: *There you go. It may not be much, but it's all we have.*
Little Girl: *Thanks.* (walks out door)
(Terry sneaks out on porch.)
Little girl: *Mom! Mom! She gave us $2 and some food! She even gave us some candy!*
(Terry comes in crying.)

It's sad when a little girl has to come to your front door asking for food for her and her little sisters and brothers. It's even sadder when people who have a lot to give won't give any, but the poorest lady would give her last dollar that she has for a week before her next $100 check.

Children can't defend themselves. They need adults to look up to. It scares me because most of these children are the ones who will be making all the violence in the year 2000. So we need to start helping now so our children will not have to worry about violence like we do.

. . .it's a million things that can happen

Freddie Owens

Chased by a Car

It was a summer night when the stars were out in the sky and the streets were very quiet.

It all happened when I was coming from over my friend's house. About 9:00 p.m., I was walking home when this car pulled up with four or five dudes inside it. It was a '79 or '80 Buick LeSabre four-door car. They pulled up beside me and they said, "Hey, you! Come here."

One of the persons rolled down the window and had something in his hand, but I couldn't see what it was.

After that happened, I ran quickly as fast as I could. I was so scared my heart was beating real fast. I just couldn't stop running. My house was right around the corner, so I ran toward my house, took my keys out of my pocket, ran up on the porch, unlocked the door, went in the house, slammed the door, and fell on the floor breathing hard.

Once I got my breath, I looked out the window and I saw the car coming out of the alley, driving around the streets looking for me. Good I made it home, but if I didn't something could have happened to me.

I was thirteen when this happened. I didn't know who they were, and I don't know why they chased me. They probably tried to start something or to mess with me. That's the worst thing that ever happened to me. Since that happened, I can't ever forget what happened that night.

You can't ever know how to survive through the streets because it's a million things that can happen.

Dusti Siefer

Terrified After School

It's really cold outside, the middle of December. I'm getting ready to leave school and walk over to my mom's friend's house to housesit. One of my friends comes up to me and we start talking about middle school and drivers ed.

Me: *Well, I really gotta go now. My mom calls every day at about 4:00 to check on me.*

Zac: *OK, I'll walk you to the doors.*

     We walk down some stairs to the doors behind the school. Up against the wall is a waist-high heater that people always sit on and talk.

Zac: *Hey, sit down a minute and talk to me.*

Me: *OK, but just for a second.*

Zac: *You're so pretty. I have a crush on you.*

Me: *Zac, you know my boyfriend and I have been going out for almost two years now.*

     I start to get my stuff together so I can go.

Zac: (pulling me towards him) *What's your hurry?*

Me: *I have to go, Zac, you know that. Let me go!*

Zac: *Can't I get a hug?*

Me: *I guess.*

     When I hug him, he picks me up and sets me on the heater.

Me: *Stop it! You're scaring me. Let me go!*

     He starts touching me and kissing me. I try to pull away. I shake my head no. But this really big, muscular, popular, football player doesn't comprehend. I try to pull his hands away from me, but he's too strong. Next thing I know he's on top of me and all I can do is whisper and cry.

Me: *No, please stop, stop, Zac, please stop.*

Zac: *You know you want me, come on baby.*

        Outside, I can see some kids getting into a car. One of them is my ex-boyfriend, and he looks over and makes eye contact with me, but he can't see the fear in my eyes. Another guy comes out and comes up to the doors. Zac gets up to open the door.

        Shaking terribly, I try to get up and get my stuff so I can hurry up and leave.

Nick: *Hey Zac, what are you guys doing?*

Zac: *Nothing.*

Nick: *Doesn't look like it.*

Zac: *Well, we're kind of busy so could you go?*

Nick looks at me: *Are you OK?*

Me: *I'm just leaving.*

Nick: *Oh.* (walking out the door)

        Zac hurries up and grabs me.

Zac: *We're not finished.*

Me: *I am, just please let me go.*

Zac: *In a minute.* (picking me up)

        I try to get out of his arms, but my attempt fails. I try to turn my face away from him so he can't kiss me, but he grabs my face and forces his tongue in my mouth, still holding my face so I can't bite him. I start to squirm so it's hard for him to touch me the way he wants to. He gets frustrated, holds me down, and gets on top of me and puts his dirty hands all over me.

        A few minutes later his brother comes down and tells Zac it's time to go.

        He jumps up real fast and leaves me there. It takes me awhile to get together but I finally get up and run home crying to call my boyfriend.

Adam Christopher Dennis

Fear of Hallways

I was walking up the long silent hallway, coming back from gym, and then all of a sudden I heard a horde of kids running down the hallway.

I wasn't sure why they were running. When I reached the end of the hallway, I saw what was going on. It was a fight!

There was a circle of kids around the two girls. It was like a bunch of vultures snapping at their prey. I couldn't see anything. There were too many kids to try to see through. When I started to walk towards the crowd of kids, the crowd started to open, and one of the girls came staggering out with dark red blood all over her face.

I was surprised that she was still walking. She lost a lot of blood. For some stupid reason, the girl turned around and went back to fight, but luckily, someone stopped her.

And then the other girl came out of the crowd handcuffed. Her shirt, which was white before, was now red from the blood of the other girl. She walked away as if it were a good thing that she had done.

And ever since that day, I sometimes hate walking down the hallways.

Eric Reader

Silence

The night is silent for a moment when I lay down in my comfortable bed.
I lie there wondering, but then screaming begins.
A high-pitched female voice screams "Stop, I'm sorry. I won't do it again."
He says, "You cheat on me, then lie about it."
First one shot, then another.
I cry myself to sleep.
Bright, hot sun wakes me. The smell in the air is strange.
Then I hear sirens, and then silence once again.

Robin Lee

Being Raped at the Age of 14

It was a cold winter day in the middle of December. The snow was falling and we had gotten out of school for it being too much on the ground. I was glad that we had gotten out because then I could sleep in longer.

At the time, I was in the eighth grade and was going out with a guy who was in the ninth grade. I had been going out with Thomas for about six months. We were having our problems, but doesn't every relationship have problems?

I wanted to tell Tommy that I was having doubts about our relationship. He had called me that morning to tell me that he was on his way over. I told him that I didn't want him to come over, that our relationship was over because I did not love him anymore and also that he was moving our relationship on a faster pace than what I wanted it to be.

He got upset with me and he hung up the phone on me. So I told myself that if he comes to my house, he won't be getting in. I then went and locked all my doors. I was determined that he was not going to be let into my house.

Well, I was right, he did come to my house. He came up to the front porch door and was pounding on the door. I told him that I was not going to let him in, but he was determined that he was going to get in.

I said to him that I wanted to break up, but he said, "Before we break up, I'm going to finish you off."

I asked him, "What are you talking about?" and he just kept repeating himself. He finally told me, while standing outside, that if I didn't let him in, he was going to make my life a living hell when I got to high school. I didn't want that to happen, so I let him into my house, thinking nothing was going to happen.

Well, I was wrong. He took me by my arms and pulled me down

to the floor in my kitchen and he raped me. I screamed for my dear life, but I knew no one could hear me scream. I tried to escape but he was forced onto me tightly and I couldn't get away. When he was done with me he left, and I just started crying, lying there.

Since that time, I have told my family, and now I don't blame myself anymore.

Jessica Willoughby

Lack of Reason

It was a summer evening. The sun was sinking behind the clouds. My mom and I had just come out of a store and were sitting in our car. The air was cool as we walked past a blue van parked next to us.
We sat for a minute as my mom started the car, and I noticed a boy, about sixteen, being held by his red flannel shirt, his father's hand gripping tightly to the shirt. I could tell something wasn't right when I saw the frightened look on the boy's face, and his father's anger evident from his body language.

My mom noticed I was looking at something that had me worried, and she turned to see. By then the dad had gotten to the blue van, opened the door, and thrown the boy inside. The father got in the back of the van where the boy covered his body, like he was preparing for a tornado. The mom sat in the driver's seat with a blank, saddened face.

I felt sick with fear. My stomach sank and cramped. My mom and I were silent. She looked at me and said to get a piece of paper and write down their license plate number. I scrambled through our cluttered glove box and pulled out a piece of paper and a pencil and wrote down the number.

As the van pulled away, my mom got out of our car and ran into the store the family had just come out of. I sat there wishing I had some super power to stop this man. My mom came back to the car, and as I looked at her I could tell she was frustrated.

She said, "I talked to the store manager and told him what we saw. At first, he wouldn't tell me anything but I convinced him that the boy was going to be hurt severely."

I looked at her and asked what the manager had said. He had told her that the boy had stolen a candy bar and had gotten caught. I looked out the window and tried to imagine the pain and fear the boy was going through now. All the way home, I tried to figure out why a person would beat another because of a stolen candy bar.

I realized how lucky I was to have parents who were not violent. I realized there was no way I would ever get out of control like that man did, because it hurts more than just the person being abused. It has an everlasting effect on people that are the victims and also on the bystanders.

Kevin Ford

Jeannie

Four years ago, I lived across the street from a family that had three children: Jeannie, age 16, Marci, age 8, and Daniel, age 7. Every day after school, Jeannie would come home and watch her brother and sister. One day when Marci got home, she came over to our house and said she couldn't get in. She didn't think Jeannie was home yet. So we waited awhile and Jeannie didn't come home.

We all got into the car and drove around looking for her. We went to all her friends' houses asking if they had seen her. We still couldn't find her. By that time, her parents had gotten home from work and we told them that we couldn't find Jeannie. Ruth, Jeannie's mother, called the school and asked if she was still there, and they said she hadn't shown up for school that day.

This went on all afternoon, looking for her. Finally we found some friends of hers who said she might be in an abandoned house a block from the school. Her parents went and looked at the house.

Late that night, they came home and everybody was crying. They told us that they found Jeannie in the house, but she had been strangled and raped. She was dead.

I remember everybody was up all night crying. About a month or so later, they caught who did it. That day, Ruth was cleaning out a closet and found one of Marci's dolls lying down in a box at the bottom of the closet. Ruth asked her why, and Marci said that Jeannie was dead.

Melissa

Verbal Violence

Small little arguments are normal for my mom and me. They happen just about every day. My whole family just considers it normal to hear my mom and me fighting every now and then. But the main thing that really emotionally bothers me is when big huge arguments occur that keep growing and growing.

I often sit and think about what I do to make my mom be upset with me and what I can do so we can just get along. I try to change my attitude towards her, I try to avoid her, and I even try to be nice to her. But somehow nothing that I try seems to work.

I also sit and wonder what my mom thinks and feels when we fight. I know that deep inside her, she loves and cares for me very much. Sometimes I wonder if she loves and cares almost too much?! Maybe she really doesn't want me to grow up and become my own independent person, not her "little girl."

This isn't a story about how someone got beat up, or shot, or hurt physically. It is about how "words can speak louder than actions." The things that my mom says to me, or about me to my face really, really hurt me on the inside, not physically.

I guess I'm just used to collecting everything up and not letting any of it out and just letting it keep building more and more up on the inside. It hurts me more to be a part of verbal violence, where it stays inside me forever in my memory, whereas physical violence such as a bruise or cut goes away with time and is healed.

Terry B. Leigh

Run Away?

Part 1

Last summer, an evil man brought together some kids to stay at his house. He lured them there by making them think it was a fun place to be. He held parties at which alcohol and marijuana were present. At first people liked him, but they didn't know him well. He let some of the kids who wanted to get away from their house live there. He started teaching them to worship the devil. The age group of kids he had living there ranged from fifteen to eighteen years of age. There were two girls and about five boys. He posed as a father to some of them.

Part 2

Sometimes, things don't go the way they are supposed to. Sometimes you just take what you have for granted. Other times you feel trapped. There are a lot of reasons a kid may want to leave home.

Once, I thought about running away. I felt like no one understood me or what it feels like to be me. I had places I could stay and be safe. I was so close to leaving, when I realized all that I had and everything I had to look forward to. Then a terrible feeling came about me. I would be leaving the people I cared most about in this world. I knew they would be devastated when they discovered I had left them. At that moment, I knew I needed someone to talk to about it. I didn't know if I could talk to my parents or not. I was afraid they would just get mad at me and think me unappreciative, but I knew it was the only way to solve this problem.

When I got around to talking to my parents, I couldn't believe how much they seemed to understand. We talked about a lot of things that needed to be talked about. Things have been much different since.

. .ran and jumped into the water,
. . . discovered he couldn't touch

Tod Martin

The Fool Cat

I know this kid named Richard who was about eleven and he lived in these apartments. It was summertime, the first time he was going to get to swim, actually the first time they opened the gate.

They all ran, except L'il Rich. He walked like he was a professional swimmer. He saw all the big kids jump in the six-foot water, so he went to the edge, looked in the water, and went back to the fence for a running start.

He paused because he saw his friends go to the shallow end. He looked puzzled. He saw his buddy do a cannonball, so he snapped out of it and ran and jumped into the water. He discovered he couldn't touch.

He panicked, splashing all the water around, screaming "Help!" So the lifeguard went after him. He was kickin' and spittin' all over the guy.

When he got to the side he threw up two fingers, signaling peace. We never saw that dude jump into deep water again.

Wayne Venik

The Shot that Never Fired

Setting:
A party, stereo playing

Characters: Thirty people talking
David: man selling gun
Jermaine: David's brother
Miles: possible buyer
Art: possible buyer

Script:
David: *Hey, man, anyone looking for some heat?* (pulls out gun)
Miles: *How much?*
David: *Fifty dollars.*
Miles: *Let me take a look?*
David: *Here you go, Dog.* (takes clip out)
Miles: *It looks tight, but I don't got enough.*
Art: *Let me peep it out.* (Miles gives gun to Art.)
Art: *How much you want for it, man?*
David: *Fifty bones.*
Art (to Miles): *You care if I buy it, Dog?*
Miles: *Hold up, Man. David, will you take 45?*
David: *Nope, I need 50.*
Miles: *Come on, Dog.*
Jermaine: (yelling) *He said 50!*
Miles: *Why you yelling, man?*
Jermaine: (still yelling) *'Cause you trying to rip us off, man.*
Miles: *That's 'cause you're chargin' too much!*

Jermaine: *What, mother #@!? (slams clip in gun) What did you say?*
Miles: *You heard me, !#@!*
Jermaine: *I'll kill you, man!* (points gun at Miles.)
Miles: *Don't aim that at me unless you got the balls to shoot.*
    (Everyone is quiet and staring at them.)
David: *What are you doin', bro? Let's bust out of here.*
    Jermaine lowers the gun and leaves with his brother.

When I saw this, I froze. It was like time stopped as soon as he aimed his gun on Miles. It made me think of how easy it is to buy a gun. If you know the right people, you can get anything you want. David was trying to sell his gun, and Miles, or anyone else in the room could have been shot and killed.

Shantell Corell

Bob and Jan

Setting:
Bedroom, late summer (August)

Characters:
Bob (16 years old) and Jan (14 years old)
(have been together for 6 or 7 months)

Script:
Bob: *I think it's a good idea. It will show me how much you love me.*
Jan: *Bob, you know I care for you a lot. I just don't think we're ready, or if I'm even ready for this. (I hope he doesn't start to get mad about this again.)*
Bob: *C'mon. Look, if you're afraid it will hurt, don't worry about it. I'll make sure you're not in any pain.*
Jan: *That's not what I'm worried about. I just am not sure if I want to.*
Bob: (yelling, very mad) *Not want to! How could you not want to? I'm your boyfriend!*
Jan: *It's not you, Bob, it's...*
Bob: (interrupting Jan, screaming) *It's the fact that you're just a little tease. I've waited almost 7 months for you and all we ever do is talk about it. It's so aggravating.*
Jan: *(oh no, here we go again) Bob, I cannot believe you think that. I can't believe you'd even say that. I'm going home. Call me after you cool down if you want, or go find some other little tease!*
Bob: *No, you're not leaving. We're not done talking.* (Bob throws Jan on the bed and continues to yell) *You don't know how much it hurts to be in my position. I deserve it after all I've been through.*
Jan: *(I really want to go home.) What you've been through! I can't believe this.* (Jan gets up and walks toward the door.) *Don't you think I feel bad? There*

is just so much stuff that can happen.
Bob: *No, it won't.*
Jan: *Sometimes I wonder if you actually even care about me.*
Bob: *I can't...Ugh! You make me so mad!*
Jan: *Call me after you cool down.*
Bob: *No, we're not done talking. Why, why do you have to tease me like this?*
Jan: *I don't tease you, I...*
Bob: (interrupting her again) *Oh, then what do you do?*
Jan: *I don't tease you.*
(Bob raises his hand and hits Jan.)
Bob: *Are we gonna or not?*
Jan: (crying from the pain) *I guess.*

As Bob forced himself on Jan, she began to cry even more. All she could hear was Bob's sister's music playing in the background. "Hero" by Mariah Carey.

Two weeks later they broke up, after another intense episode like this one.

Dustin Fremion

Gun At School

One time I was in seventh grade and one of my friends brought a gun to school. I knew he had it, but I wasn't going to tell on him, because I knew he wouldn't do anything to me, so I wasn't scared.

I found out around third period, and then slowly the word started to spread. Pretty soon kids that didn't even know Brent were finding out about it. Brent soon found out and had to think of something fast. He saw Ken in the hall and told Ken to take the gun on the bus. Ken said all right and Brent thought he was free.

The bell rang and kids filed out of classrooms. Brent strolled out and saw Mr. Archer, the I.S.S. teacher, who was cool and got along well with students. Archer walked up and said "What's up, Brent?" and gave him five. But Archer didn't let go, he grabbed Brent and kept asking him where the gun was.

Brent denied it and was released. Later, on the bus, Ken was scared, so he passed it to R.J.

Interested, but not scared, I watched all of this in front of my eyes. But there was no reason to tell on my friends, because nothing would have happened to me. After this, nothing was different. It wasn't the first time a gun was brought to my middle school.

I guess if someone got shot that day, I would have felt a little guilty, but all of my friends got along with him so nothing would have happened.

Shacara Cortese Henley

Will It Ever End?

I was walking down the hall with my best friend on a day like any other day in school: loud, noisy, people talking. It smelled really bad because someone had set off a stink bomb in the hall.

As we were walking, a girl walked up to my best friend and started talking to her. Then she began to get very loud. She was arguing with my best friend about her going out with her ex-boyfriend.

All of a sudden, we were all crowded. It seemed like the whole school was around us. Then her friends started calling my friend bad names. I began to get really upset because they were trying to jump her.

My first thought was loyalty to my friend, so I wasn't going to let them fight. I didn't want my friend to get kicked out of school. I tried to tell the girl it wasn't worth fighting over, and that my friend didn't want to fight.

She didn't pay me any attention, and she struck my best friend. Then her three other friends jumped her.

My first reaction was panic. So I simply just fought too. In the end, it was two on four and the two came out on top. No one was seriously hurt, just a few cuts, bruises and black eyes.

I know it was wrong to fight, and I don't like fighting, but I couldn't let her fight that battle alone. I love her with all my heart, and I cherish her, and I can't say that about too many people.

Good loyal friends are hard to come by.

Big Man

Beware

I can remember it like it happened yesterday. It was a humid Saturday, around 9:30 P.M. Me and a couple of my boys were sitting on my porch, listening to "Live and Die in L.A.," drinking some beer, and smoking some bud.

Everybody was bored, so we called some girls. The girls were about to come by, so we changed to slow music. The girls all had boyfriends, but they didn't care, so we didn't either.

About 10 or 15 minutes later, the girls pulled up. Nobody noticed the slow-moving car coming down the street. The car parked about three houses down, so we didn't pay it much attention.

We sat in my house for about half an hour, just talking and listening to music. The girls had to make a run, and told us they would be right back. So me being a nice guy, I walked them to the car.

I started to give one a kiss, and I heard tires screaming. I took one look and jetted toward my front door. Pow! Pow! Pow! Like three firecrackers. I dove on the ground and grabbed my hip. It felt like someone had burned me with a lighter.

The blood was pouring like a waterfall. The car never stopped. It took off around the corner.

I was so scared that I passed out. When I woke up, I saw everyone standing around crying. My mom was hysterical.

My injury was a minor graze wound to the hip. A couple of days later I found out that the dude who did it was a jealous boyfriend.

At first I was thinking about payback, but now after really thinking about it, I just let it go. I don't really want to lose my life over some female.

And after this incident, I decided to stop smoking bud and only drink occasionally.

Steven M. Ramsey

Nowhere's Safe

Many people think churches, church groups, and other activities are safe places where nothing really bad can happen. Well that's wrong—even church-related things can go bad.

About three weekends ago, a local youth group that many students from our school go to planned a "lock-in" at the middle school. A lock-in is a big sleepover with planned activities such as tourneys, talent shows and movies.

But the trouble started outside just before we went in. The weekend before, a small dispute had happened when I flicked someone off for throwing trash out the window and almost hitting my friend's truck. They took it too seriously and it almost caused them to be killed or injured. They saw all of us at the lock-in and felt like causing some trouble.

Up until that point, the night was warm, with clear skies and everyone was in a good mood. But quickly, the night seemed to get an icy chill to it, and there was an air of fear and tension as the kids pulled into the parking lot.

Since I was the one who gave them the finger, they called me over to the car. Our two groups have a strong dislike for each other, almost like rival gangs. Jim asked me why I flicked him off, and amazingly enough, we got things cleared up quickly. Or so I thought.

I thought things were finished and they were going to leave, but as they were leaving, one of my friends cursed at them and threw his cigarette at their car. My friends and I knew what was about to happen. Their car stopped really fast and three of them jumped out and came right up to us.

That was their big mistake, because one of my friends, Jeremy, is friends with one of the larger gangs, and some gang members were there. When the three guys from the car got up in everyone's faces, Jeremy's friend, John, walked up to them holding up his 9mm.

"Unless you get back in your car and leave right now, I'll shoot all three of you," he said.

Jim and his friends tried to act like they were not worried, but we could see the color drain from their faces. It was silent for a moment, and then my friend and I said at the same time, "John, put the gun away."

Jeremy said, "Jim, turn and leave now. He's not lying when he says he will shoot."

Jim said, "Fine, but you better stop speaking about us that way." He said that to keep some pride. Then they all turned, got in their car, and sped off quickly.

John put up the gun. We all laughed at how they tried not to run in fear or wet their pants. Then we all turned and went inside. The rest of the night was fun and problem free.

Lucas Foster

My Brother Gets Arrested

I don't quite remember the exact day it was when my brother got arrested. It was sometime in early December of '95.

I'd known for some time that my brother had become friends with two brothers from Fort Wayne, Freddy and Joe. Freddy was real nice. He talked to us a lot when he came over. Joe didn't come around much. Travis (my brother) started hanging more with Joe and a group of his friends. Travis started talking and dressing different. He always wore black pants with a plaid shirt with only the top button buttoned up. He fought with my parents a lot.

The night before he was arrested was a normal night. Travis called home from Kroger's supermarket where he had gone to get an application. He said he had slipped in some mud on his way out and was going to a friend's house to change his clothes, but would be home shortly.

When he got home, his clothes were covered in mud, but he was in a very good mood. The next morning he went to school as usual and so did my younger brother and I. The rest of that day was normal. It was an overcast, rainy day so my mom picked my younger brother and I up from school and drove us home.

About an hour later there was a knock on our door. I opened it and there was a police officer standing there. He asked me if my mother was home and I said no. He asked me to call her and have her come home.

Then that same officer asked me some questions. He said, "Have you ever seen your brother with any guns at home?" and I said, "No."

Then he asked, "Have you seen any of his friends with guns?" and again I said, "No."

After that, my mom drove me to my parents' friend's house, and

I stayed there for the next day.

The thing I remember the most about that day was opening the door and hearing police scanners and police dogs barking.

My brother had joined a gang and got arrested for stealing guns. He was muddy because he had slipped while running across a field. He was in such a good mood because they had gotten away with it. He was arrested that day while I was at school. The police had come to search my house but found nothing.

Since then, my family has been in debt with lawyer's fees and court costs, and our reputation has been ruined. When some people hear my name, they think of my brother, and if they don't know me, they just assume I'm like him. He's a good person if you know him. He just made a few mistakes. Since then my family hasn't been able to live our lives the way we'd like to, but we get along all right.

. . .if we let it hurt us, it's hard to live,
it's hard to survive.

Chelsea Cella

Why Darkness Seems So Light

It was the summer before my sophomore year, and I was with all my girls at a party downtown—keg outside, people playing spades in the kitchen, people dancing in another room, people getting high upstairs and outside. This party was in a different part of town than the parties we usually go to, but my friend Vera knew the fellow having the party. We invited some of our dudes from our school, Brad, Stacy, Bee, and Rory. No one, from what me and the girls have seen, could or would step to them.

But I guess we were wrong. Every party we go to, there is a ruckus (or fight), so it's not a big deal, but this time I overheard some dudes talking about jumping my friends. So I tried to find my friends to tell them to bust. I had felt the tension building up to this, and I knew the dudes were looking for them.

I was too late. It had already started when I found them. I was helpless in this situation. I wanted to help them, but I couldn't. I'm just some girl, and my friends and I were outnumbered. It happened so fast, I couldn't even think about what I could do.

About half the party turned to Brad. His boys stood by him, and then about 6 or 7 dudes from another school surrounded them. Brad tried to get them to back off, but they wouldn't.

Meanwhile, a new guy showed up. I saw him fighting with some dudes. A couple of them pulled out their strap (gun), so I pulled my friends and ran. We found Brad and the others, and a few minutes later we all drove by the party. I thought the fighting would be all over, but it wasn't.

We saw police cars and yellow tape. A couple of hours later, I found out that someone at the party was shot and killed. He was shot in the arm and it punctured his lung, killing him. It was sad, in fact very sad, but most people acted like it was nothing, which made me even more upset.

Everyone knows you have to hide your feelings. Well, everyone is led to believe that; it's a form of defense. People, children, my friends, me...if we let it hurt us, it's hard to live, it's hard to survive.

Danielle Hilworth

Death in His Eyes

Have you ever looked into the eyes of someone who has watched someone die? There's something there that no one else has. Their eyes have lost their innocence and their souls have hardened. But still underneath, there's that little child inside crying because he has been shut away.

I have a close friend. His name is John. When we first met, he goofed off a lot, but as we spent long nights talking he surprised me by opening up. At first he would tell me about his childhood, and how he grew up in a rough neighborhood. As we got even closer, we would meet to talk and I started to notice something in his brown eyes. I could see the pain from his past that he kept secret. Then he started to tell me about his best friend, Matt.

John was fifteen, Matt twenty. They were leaving a shopping center together to go wherever they ended up. John told me he heard a single gunshot, then all of a sudden, Matt just collapsed in an alley behind the mall. There was nothing he could do but hold him while he died. And that is exactly what he did. John said it felt like hours as Matt lay in his arms bleeding to death and coughing up blood. The gunshot must have punctured his lungs.

John cried that day. But as Matt took his last breath and John lay him down on the cold ground, he stood up, wiped away his last tear, and disappeared. When you grew up where they grew up, there were givens. It was a silent pact among friends.

If John were to stay there, and the cops would show up, they would have to question him. Then John would get hit with questions like: Who is Matt? What did he do to get shot? Why would someone kill him? How are you involved with him? These are questions that could get John and other acquaintances of Matt in trouble, and that is just something you don't do.

John and his friends have their own set of rules and you see them being enforced whenever you hear about a drive-by or finding someone dead in a parking lot alley like Matt. Everyone who lives by those rules has the cold spot in their eyes and soul, and if you don't stay cold, you'll melt and die.

And, God, never show fear. That is the worst thing you can do, and if someone who hates senses your fear, you're dead. Hatred, coldness and fearlessness are what you need to live by to survive. It's sad but true.

So, John told me, that night there was no one to tell, nothing to do but forget. But as I sat there and looked into his eyes, something told me he never forgot.

Now don't get me wrong. John's not all ice. He tries to be. He does what he can to not get attached to anything for fear he's going to get hurt, but the more we're together, the more I see him letting go and letting me in. I feel it whenever we're together, and so does he, so he is scared again.

Eyes are definitely the doorway to a person's soul.

Porscha Davis

A Miracle

It was around July, and my cousin and I were outside clowning. We were just talking about everything. One of the topics was how we have all grown in my family and another topic was about my father.

"He never really cared," I said.

Steve said, "Porscha, we all know how your father is, and although he lies to you and doesn't do anything for you, he still loves you, and he will never stop his love for you."

Although I had a lot of anger for my dad, I knew Steve was right. He gave me a hug and said, "I love you like my sister. You have to overlook all the bad things about people you love, and see the good things. Your father has a problem, and you know how his drinking affects how he acts, so you have to be strong and forgive him. My father has never been there either, but one day they will see and regret it and nothing is worse than knowing your child is grown and you weren't there to watch them grow or help them with their good and bad times."

I gave Steve a kiss on the cheek and told him that I appreciated how he always helped me with my problems. "It's like you know all the answers when it comes to my father."

He said, "Boo, I love your father, and although he has some problems and he's not doing his job, he does love you, and if you give him time, he will get better, hopefully, with his life, and your relationship with each other. Just pray. God will answer your prayers."

I said, "Thank you, Steve. I love you, and take care of yourself, because when I come back for Christmas, we will have to party!" He said the same to me, and I left.

When I arrived on Christmas, I asked my cousin where Steve was, and she paused.

I said, "Hello. Can you hear me? Where is Steve?"

She said, "Porscha, he got shot in the back like five times, about a month ago."

I said, "Swear to God?"

She said, "I swear."

I started crying because he meant a lot to me, and I said, "Is he dead?"

"No, but he is paralyzed from the neck down and can't talk."

"Where is he?" I asked.

She told me, and I went to see him. His eyes were closed and he was just resting in the bed. He couldn't talk so I talked to him. I told him that I loved him and I would pray for him every day until he was well.

I couldn't stay too long because I knew my pain would grow just watching him lying in a hospital bed, so I left after giving him a kiss. I cried, but that's all I could do.

I went to my grandparents' house where he lived and talked to them. I asked who did it, and they said no one knew who did it or why, but it's done.

I started to cry, not sorrow, but anger because nothing is worth destroying someone else's life.

Later, I went back home and I found out that he was out of the coma, and he could talk again. They said he'd still be paralyzed, but at least he was alive!

Added, two months later:

Just last Sunday, I went with my father and Steve's brother to visit him and he was doing real well. Today he is coming back down here from Warsaw. He will be in the hospital, and he's going through therapy. By the end of this year, we hope he will be walking!

. . .I began to feel a pain
I never wanted to feel

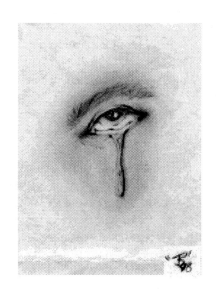

Latoya Baker

Our First Meeting Was Our Last

When I was about eleven years old, I met my cousin Charles "Delvon" Anspach, for the first time. It was a nice summer day and we were all outside playing football when he picked me to be on his team. Later we took pictures together and he gave me a hug and a kiss on the cheek and told me it was nice meeting me.

Two years went past and I didn't hear from him, until one day my great aunt called me and told me Delvon had got hurt. My heart dropped. They wanted me to go to the hospital, but it was too depressing. I just stayed home and prayed that he would be allright. Around 9:00 they called and told me there was no hope. He was gone. A gunshot wound to the head was all it took, and there was no one to blame because he pulled the trigger himself.

At his funeral, I couldn't cry because I barely knew him, but he was very special. I really felt sorry for his girlfriend because she was carrying their child. Now she has to explain to little Delvana what a great father she would have had.

When we went to bury him, I suddenly had flashbacks of my brother who had died eight months before Delvon died. I became light-headed and cold myself. I suddenly began to feel a pain I never wanted to feel, the pain of grief.

I went on grieving in very weird ways—what did I have to lose? I already lost my brother and my cousin in one year. I didn't know how to handle it. I was only thirteen years old. I started looking at things in a totally different way. I became somewhat rebellious! I couldn't help it, it seemed like the only way.

I wish there was something I could have done to save both of them, but it wasn't in my hands. It was in God's hands. For a long time

I thought he made the wrong choice; he took the wrong people. But I had to grow up and learn that everything happens for a reason.

I still miss them, but I have my own life to live. I have to make sure the same thing doesn't happen to me. Anthony and Delvon will forever be in my heart, but I have to move on.

Jennifer Schimmoller

A Trip That Turned Tragic

It was in late May about two years ago when my youth group leaders, Dan and Sarah Jones, decided to take the youth from my church to see a Christian concert. We had an early dismissal from school that day, so we were all in really good moods.

We all went in one van. Sarah, my friend Sandi, and I were all in the back seat talking about school, and guys, just kind of girl talk. We got to the concert, then headed home.

Sarah was in a really good mood. She was talking and laughing a lot. Then we dropped Sarah off at our church so that she could drive herself home. Dan, her husband, stayed with the kids, as he drove us all home individually.

It was around 10:00 p.m. Sarah pulled in her driveway. A man came up to her window, apparently to just scare her, when something went wrong. She was shot six times in the chest and was all alone dying.

When Dan got home around 10:45, he noticed that the windows in his car were broken out. He got out of his car and peered through the window. There he saw his wife covered in blood and barely alive. She was now in the passenger's side of the car, and all of the doors were locked.

Dan called 911 and waited for the ambulance. He was helpless. He stood in the silence watching his wife die. The ambulance came but it was too late. Sarah died on the way to the hospital.

My friend called me the next morning. "Did you hear what happened to Sarah last night? She was murdered." I sat down on my bed and started to cry. It couldn't be true.

The next day at church, our youth group had a meeting. It was true. All the kids began to cry and ask questions.

Well, why didn't someone call for help? Apparently the neighbors heard gunshots but because it was dark, they decided they shouldn't go out.

After everything happened, the same question stuck in every kid's mind: If we wouldn't have gone on this trip, would she still be alive today?

Brea Lesley

Goodbye

I sit in the darkness and hold his picture close to my heart. Tears stream down my face. I look out my window and glance at the moon. It has that unusual paleness I've seen before. I close my eyes and my mind takes me back.

"Dear father, I ask tonight for you to forgive my sins. I also ask for protection against the harsh world. Give me the strength to overcome any hardships I shall endure. Amen."

I awoke that morning with a sense of peacefulness. School was great, everything was going my way. How was I to know my life would be changed forever in a matter of hours?

I laid my head down and prayed to God, waiting to dream. *My mind slips in and out of subconsciousness. I can picture my youngest brother in my head, and that seems odd.*

The phone rings and I hear screams and cries of disbelief in my head. I awake suddenly to find the cries are real, and the image of him in my head slips away.

"Dad? What's wrong?" I shouted out. I looked out the window before descending to the living room. *The moon is an unusual pale tonight. As I turn the corner, fear strikes my heart.*

I see my dad in his blue shirt lying on the floor cradling the phone, barely making a sound through his cries. I rush to his side to hear what has happened.

I remember asking Dad if it was Mom. He shook his head no, and I knew instantly who it was. My beautiful blond-haired brother. The one I had known my whole life. The one I taught how to ride a bike. *What sadness has caused this?*

It took forever to get to the hospital that night. I remember looking at the houses along the road with their lights on. *How dare they have a normal night, while mine is shattered?*

We walked through the doors to the hospital and it was there I found my little brother. I also found the answers to my questions. It was there I mourned my loss.

I look back on it now and wonder what might have been. He was so talented. I remember cheering him on at games. He made us all so proud. So much talent that will forever be wasted.

Had he known the sadness and pain, maybe he'd never have pulled the trigger. He'd still be here making us all laugh and smile.

I say goodbye to you now little brother. I'll see you when my life is complete. Your troubles may be over, but for the ones who love you, ours have just begun.

Everyone looks through different windows Adam, and I'm sorry I couldn't protect you from what you saw outside yours.

Brandon Jordan

Artia

On January 11th, 1998, violence really affected me in a bad way when my cousin and one of her unborn twins were killed at her apartment in Village Park. She was a very important part in my life because she was always there for me. She was like my sister.

Her name was Artia Sha'Marr Cooper-Causey. She was only twenty years old when she was killed. It really hurt me a lot because the night before she was murdered, I was around the corner from her apartment and I was going to go and spend the night with her but I didn't. I used to blame myself and sometimes I still do, because I wonder if I had gone over to her house that night, would she have died, or would I have been able to save her?

Also killed was her unborn son, La'Shawn Ra'Shad Cooper-Causey. Her son that survived is Ti'Shawn Christian Cooper Causey (now 2 months old), and her oldest son is Brandon La'Shawn Dock (2 years old). I treat them both like they were my nephews and I'd do anything for them, just like their mother did for me.

All I want to say is guns and violence are not a joke, and if you have to carry a gun, carry for the right reason, protection, not just to hurt people.

Rest in Peace, Tia. We'll miss you.

Artia Sha'Marr Cooper-Causey
1977-1998

Michelle J. Penn

One Night Changed my Life Forever

October 19, 1996 is a day I will never forget for as long as I live.

It was a warm autumn night in a city where I used to live, in Ohio. Everything started around 7:00 p.m. It was a Saturday night, and the day before, my best friend, Tyrone, got a new car. I had heard about a party on the "West Side" of town. I brought it up to Tyrone and he said he didn't want to go, simply because we lived on the "East Side." He thought that it wouldn't be a good idea for the "Easts" to be going to a "Wests" party. All he kept saying was "No. Hell, no."

I begged and begged. It finally got on his nerves so he gave in and said "yes" but only until 12:30 a.m. I was so excited to go. I threw on my new outfit, which I will never forget. My new white Tommy shirt, with my new jeans, and of course my all white Nikes. I was so excited to go out with Tyrone and go to a West Side's party.

We finally left and we were on our way. It was about a 20-minute drive. It seemed like it lasted forever. Tyrone kept saying, "You know we shouldn't go. You know your dad will be mad if he finds out it's out west."

All I could say was, "Shut up, everything's fine. We ain't got nothing to worry about." Ignoring the bad feeling about the whole thing, I didn't care. I just wanted to go.

Tyrone said, "If anything happens it's your fault."

When we arrived at the party, we heard music playing and people laughing and yelling and all I could think was "Yes, we are here!" I looked over at Tyrone. He was looking underneath his seat for his 9mm. His gun. And I yelled, "Damn it, Ty, put that away. Someone could see you with that. You won't even need it."

Feeling bad, he looked at me and said, "Sorry," and put it back underneath the seat.

We got out of the car and we immediately recognized our friends from our neighborhood, sitting on the front porch. Greetings were exchanged with a few handshakes representing our neighborhood, "East," and throwing up the gang sign. That's what started the whole thing.

That night changed my life forever. I never imagined the outcome.

I never even stepped a foot in the party. Tyrone and I sat down to talk to our friends on the front porch. An all black Jeep Cherokee with black tinted windows pulled up across the street. The people in the Jeep just sat there for a few minutes. The driver rolled down the window and said "Ain't y'all from East?"

Ty's friends quickly yelled, "Yeah...why, who wants to know?"

The driver jumped out of his seat and ran over to us. Words were exchanged from the two sides. The guys from the Jeep ran over to Tyrone and his friends. All I could do was sit there hoping someone wouldn't get hurt, and frantically yelling, "Stop!"

Tyrone was in the middle of the street, fighting with some guy. The guy was short and cocky, very muscular. He looked really mean. He just looked at Ty with the evilest eyes and kicked him in the stomach. All Tyrone could do was lie on the ground. He kept trying to get up but he couldn't get up to his knees. Ty finally got up and bum-rushed the man. The guy got really mad and reached into his pocket and pulled out his gun.

Everything stopped. Everyone's eyes were on the guy (now the gunman) . Everything was frozen. I could hear the trees rustle in the breeze and the ice cream truck across the street. Then there was a loud pop. Everyone ducked to hide. Tyrone stood there holding his chest. I looked around. All his friends ran.

"Tyrone," I screamed, "He's been shot! Call 911!" I ran over to hold Tyrone in my arms. Looking into his eyes, I could see fear like I have never seen before. It scared me.

There was blood everywhere. It ran down the street gutter like rain water and rolled down the sewer. It seemed like forever until the ambulance finally showed. I heard the sirens and said, "Baby, it's gonna be ok. Trust me."

He looked at me and said, "Please don't cry. It's gonna be ok." As soon as the paramedics came over, his eyes shut and his body fell limply. All I could do was scream and cry.

To this day, I still feel guilty, even after going through therapy for almost two years. It all would've changed and been better if I just hadn't asked.

I'm sorry Ty. R.I.P. I love you.

Tony Barnhart

Pain

It all started with Mike and one of the kids who rushed us. I don't know how it started. I don't really remember how it ended. I just remember pulling this dude off Mike, and then punching him in his throat and him falling to his knees. Then I kicked him in his stomach. He folded up after that.

I looked at my friends and myself beating these kids. Then the kid at my feet tried to get up. I snapped back in and started to kick in his face.

After we ran and got to Josh's house, we were hyped and glad. But that night I thought hard before I fell asleep. I thought, if that was me? If that was my pain, and what was the reason for fighting?

. . .I can't live in one terrible moment
the rest of my life.

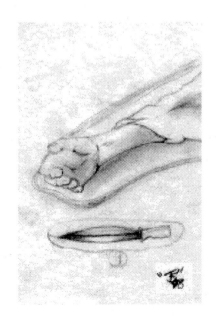

Elisabeth Andrews

One Terrible Moment

"You can't live in one terrible moment the rest of your life," my mother often told me, until I was twelve, when I lost her. I think of this now as I hold her white blouse with crimson blood stains sprayed mostly on the lace. The perfume that my mother always wore drifts to my nose bringing back the vivid memories I often try to forget.

My mother was a short, petite Italian woman with great beliefs in strength, courage, and faith. Her only problem was that she was too strong, too courageous, and too faithful. She was so faithful that she couldn't leave my stepfather who repeatedly beat us both. She was so courageous that she gave her life to save her daughter from her own husband's anger. She was so strong she couldn't recognize the pain most individuals could not endure. Her spirit still lives in the hearts of many she's touched emotionally.

I remember the afternoon she died as if it were yesterday. It was the seventh day of September and it was slightly overcast outside. My mother had just come home from work and wore her light blue business suit and white blouse trimmed with lace. Her long, curly, dark brown hair was up as usual and she would've looked beautiful if it weren't for the dull look of sadness that lingered in her dark brown eyes.

My stepfather abruptly stormed out of the kitchen and grabbed me by my hair, viciously yanking me to the kitchen. Still pulling hard, he yelled that I hadn't finished the dishes. I remember the smell of alcohol on his breath. Though I apologized, he began slapping me over and over.

I heard my mother's footsteps and loud voice as she burst into the kitchen and tried to stop him. He flung her off him effortlessly and his endless cursing drowned out her voice. I watched him go from the kitchen to the couch. He opened the second drawer of the end table and pulled out a shiny black gun.

The fear I felt wouldn't allow my voice to break loose and warn my mother. I watched every action of her murder. Then, I watched my stepfather shoot himself in the head. I tried to save my mother, but nothing I could do would revive her, so I pulled her close and cried on the white blouse, holding her for the last time, taking in her fragrance.

Sometimes I find myself blaming the incident on myself. Sometimes I find myself crying in the middle of the night, and wishing I would've finished the dishes. And sometimes I wish I had my best friend to discuss the incident with, but I remember that I don't. My stepfather took the life of my best friend.

As long as I live, I'll carry on my mother's beliefs, but I'll never be too strong, too courageous, or too faithful, or too careful. As long as I live, I'll always keep the image of my mother in the back of my mind, but when I remember the incident, I'll also remember that I can't live in one terrible moment the rest of my life.

Janita M. Crandall

My Friend and her Sister

It was a very cool day in February. There was just enough snow on the ground so you couldn't see the green grass.

My best friend's mom had to work that day, just as she did every day. She was a very hard worker, and has always had to work very hard to take care of her two daughters. She didn't graduate from high school, had a very low paying job, and struggled to have the best of everything for my friend.

What I didn't know about her is that she was so stressed out, she was taking it out on my friend and her little sister.

My friend was the oldest of the two girls, so she got beat the worst. I guess it was also because whenever she was allowed to go somewhere she always got in some kind of trouble. Then her mom would punish her by beating her. My friend's little sister would try lying for her, and then she would get beat too.

But one day their mother got carried away. She was pulling my friend's hair with all of her strength, sitting on her chest and choking her and then trying to beat her with a big wooden paddle anywhere possible. The younger sister, age nine, was crying and wanted to call the police, but she didn't want her mom to go to jail.

The older sister, age fourteen, was crying and screaming "Mom, Mom, please stop! It hurts!" Finally her mother stopped, after she hadn't heard her daughter say anything for awhile. My friend was lying in the middle of the living room floor, bleeding, not breathing and not moving.

Their mother didn't know what to do so she began smacking her daughter in the face and telling her to quit playing and do something.

Finally, my friend started to breathe again. Her mother grabbed her and began crying and rocking her and promising that she would change. They both sat there crying while the younger daughter hid in the closet so her mother wouldn't hurt her.

Finally, the weekend had passed, and the two girls went back to school. That day in school, all of us girls were in the restroom and my friend started showing all of us her bruises. Five minutes later the bell rang and everyone went back to their classes except for me and another friend.

We went to the office and told the principal about what had happened. He called my friend to the office, and when she walked in, he could see the hurt and pain she was in. Bruises and welts were everywhere.

His assistant called child protective services and they picked my friend up at school. They also went and got her little sister, and called their mother to make her aware of the fact. She couldn't believe what she was hearing, but it was all real.

The older daughter ended up in a children's home and the younger one in a foster home.

This all made their mother realize what she was doing to her children. After one weekend the younger daughter was released back to her mother. My friend stayed in the children's home for a year and a half and then went back with her mother.

Their mother has gone to counseling by herself and with her children and is now a changed person. She won't even play hit or anything, with her daughters.

Matt Kissinger

The Last Drive

I remember that it was a nice day. The sun was shining, the grass was green, and I was in school. Most of the day was still to come, and I was looking forward to getting out and playing football with my friends at the vacant lot, like we did every Friday.

I heard my name over the P.A. system. It told me that I had an appointment to go to, and that I should go to the office.

I saw my stepmother there, waiting. She told me we were going to see my real mother because she was in some kind of accident. My sister approached and I told her the news. I must say, I was happy. It had been awhile since I had seen my mother; after all, she lived in Chicago, Illinois, and my dad moved us here to Fort Wayne, Indiana.

So the only time I got to see her and the rest of her side of the family was on holidays. My brother still lived with our mom because he and my stepmother never really got along.

The car ride was long; it takes about three and a half hours to drive there, and every minute felt like an eternity. We were not given very many details about what had happened, so our minds were left to wander, and my imagination roamed.

I remember imagining my mom with a broken leg or something along those lines. Maybe her head would be bandaged, but through all that she would still have a smile, and she'd greet us with hugs and long-awaited kisses. I imagined that we would just sit and talk for hours about the stuff that had happened since the last time we had seen each other. I was very happy that I was going to see my mother.

The car ride seemed to take the longest time. It went on forever. All of a sudden, my happy thoughts faded. I began to imagine what it would be like if everything wasn't ok. But I quickly pushed those thoughts away and reassured myself that everything was ok. It was at that time I prayed for her to be all right.

We weren't very far now. I was getting excited. When we pulled up to the hospital, I noticed that the day had turned from being nice and bright to being cold and dark. I didn't give it much thought; my mind was on finally seeing my mom.

We walked into the waiting room to find that my aunt and uncle were waiting down there instead of upstairs in my mom's room. Looking back on the moment, I can remember my aunt's facial expression. It wasn't her usual happy, energetic appearance. Instead, she looked sad, and almost apologetic. The thought crossed my mind that maybe it was because she had something to do with the accident.

My sister and I were next led into a small room just down the hall from the waiting room. The room consisted of a couch, a coffee table, and a box of tissues on the table. I didn't want to be in there. I knew that the only thing in there was bad news. I asked when we would be able to see her, and nobody answered. A cold chill went up my back. I knew what was coming.

Then my dad finally said it, "Kids, I have bad news. Your mom died." They explained that she was driving home from the bar with her boyfriend; they had been drinking and an argument started. According to him, she jumped out of his truck while it was speeding down the road. But I never believed it. I believe that he pushed her out. He had always been abusive toward her. There had been times when we weren't able to visit her because he had beaten her up. She didn't want us seeing her like that.

My mom's name is Hope. She was a loving, caring woman. She was always there when times were hard, when everything felt like it was coming undone. She taught us to keep our heads up, and most important, she taught us never to give up hope. As long as I can remember her, she will forever be in my heart and in my dreams. I know one day we will meet again, and we will be together forever, as long as I keep up my hopes.

Kevin D. Jones

Awkward Position

Three years ago, I was working at a restaurant. It was a Sunday afternoon, and we were busy. As I was walking back to the dish room, my manager motioned that there was a phone call for me. I picked it up, and to my surprise, it was my father on the other end. The reason I was surprised was because I don't normally talk to my dad, and that was the last person I would have expected to be receiving a phone call from at work.

My parents got a divorce that was final during the summer before my sixth grade year. We never had a strong father/son relationship, and that was always a factor in my reasoning for not maintaining a close relationship after the divorce. We never went fishing, never played catch, never watched "the big game" together, or anything else that I always expected should happen in a family setting.

I am the middle child in the family. I have a sister who is twenty, a brother who is ten, and I am seventeen. Keeping even a hint of attention on myself was hard to do, and normally the only way I could get my parents to acknowledge my existence on the planet was to get into trouble. That wasn't something that I strived for, but occasionally that's how things went.

My sister set the way for me throughout school, and naturally my parents thought that I should follow in her footsteps. She was on the Honor Roll ever since she was in the grade that it started, and she graduated in '95 with an Honors Diploma. But my road to success in school wasn't paved with gold as was hers. I am a B-C student, and throughout my schooling years, my grades have fluctuated for the better sometimes, but also for the worse.

Anyway, my dad asked me if I had a second to talk, and after verifying it with my manager, I responded with a yes. He said that he was following some recipe, and that one of the ingredients called for beer. He noted that other alcohols would enhance the flavor too, but he figured that beer might be more easily accessible. My dad is of German descent, and I remembered that many German recipes called for beer and the like. I knew that he never drank, so the possibility of using the alcohol for anything other than his recipe hadn't even entered my mind.

He asked me if we had anything at my house he could use, alcohol-wise, and knowing that my mom didn't drink either, nor was anyone else old enough to drink there, I thought something was fishy. I wondered also why he hadn't simply called my house to talk to my mom, but I didn't think too much about it.

I said no, answering his question, and then asked one of my own. I asked why he didn't just go buy some, not thinking about it being a Sunday. He said that you couldn't buy alcohol on Sunday in Indiana, which I already knew but had ceased to remember, and he didn't want to drive all the way to Ohio. We said our goodbyes, and I figured it was over, but it had only begun.

About 3:30 the next morning, I was unwantedly awakened by the sound of the telephone. I knew after one ring that my mom had answered it. About five minutes later she came into my room, turned on the light and sat on a chair in the corner of the room. She said that my dad had tried to commit suicide. He failed in his effort, but was at Lutheran Hospital for the next two days.

When I asked my mom several days later how it happened, she said he swallowed a bunch of pills and then emptied the wet bar at my sister's house into his stomach. Apparently a neighbor reported a man struggling to walk through my sister's front lawn, which is where my dad lived at the time. When the authorities arrived, my dad was passed out on the porch.

Needing information regarding who my father was, they entered into the house. They came to where my sister and who is now my brother-in-law were asleep with their two children. They awoke them and asked them to identify the man on the porch, and it was my father. Then the police called for an EMS, and the night was over.

The reason that this brought me to where I am today in terms of where I stand with my dad is because in my mind, being asked to get him supplies that would have made it possible for him to take his life would have made me an accomplice to his death. To me that would be a terrible thing to have to carry for the rest of my life, and for him to put me in a position like that seemed and still seems messed up. That is why I felt I was put into an "awkward position."

Rhett Ford

My Brother's Birthday

It was Friday, April 26, my brother's birthday. I had just gotten home from school, and told my mom of the plans I had for the night. She told me that I couldn't go anywhere because we were going to a family movie.

I said, "Mom, I don't want to go to a movie with my family on a Friday night when you never told me that we were going and we can go any other night."

She said she didn't care, that I was going. She also said that as soon as we got back from the movie, I could go out with my friends.

I went to the movie with my parents after a lot of arguing and complaining because I had no prior knowledge of their plans. On the way out from the movie, I saw many people I knew, and they made fun of me for going to the movies with my parents.

When I got home, my friend called and asked me if I wanted to go bowling. I told him I would call him back in a minute. I went up to ask my parents if I could go bowling and they said no because I argued about going to the movies.

I told them they were not being fair to me. My dad replied, "I've had enough of your back talk," and smacked me in the face. I just stood there and stared him straight in the eye. He smacked me again, and again I didn't move.

This seemed to make him mad, because he wasn't hurting me, so he punched me this time. My mom screamed a terrible cry, and I saw blood squirt on the nice white carpet. I covered my lip and walked into the bathroom.

My lip was four times its normal size and was cut very deep, because at the time I had braces. I washed out my mouth and gargled with water. Finally, the blood slowed down and I went to my room and angrily listened to music. The past hour had gone so fast that I hadn't had time to think about what had happened.

I guess at first I was surprised at what happened. I had not used any foul language or said anything mean to set my dad off, so I don't really know why he did it. We had gotten into many arguments of the same intensity before, but he had never hit me.

Since then, my father hasn't hit me. For about two weeks after that happened, I said nothing to him. But every night before I went to bed he said, "I'm sorry."

The only things I have left from that day are memories and a scar on my upper lip.

Alyssa

Almost Dead

She held the sharp, shiny, deadly object in her hand, moving her finger up and down the blade, the blade she was planning to take her life with.

Although it was a beautiful day outside, she didn't notice. Her mind was concentrated on only one thing: her problems. Alone in her bedroom, she replayed the past few months of her life: her friends, her ex-boyfriend, her mom, everything that had gone wrong.

She thought of the day, not long ago, when she and her best friend had had their first fight. That had also been a beautiful day, but because of her anger and stubbornness, she hadn't noticed.

She sat there feeling the blade of her knife, going over in her mind what it would be like with no problems. Alone. Dead. Her heart was beating faster than it had ever gone. She was more nervous than she had ever been.

Although she hadn't said goodbye to anyone, she had written a note to her mom and her best friends, and a poem for her ex-boyfriend. She knew they would understand. Her confidence was at a high just as the sun set.

She didn't know how long she had been sitting there, but she knew she was ready. She wanted to test the waters, so she made a small incision on her left wrist. She felt nothing but relief. She felt no pain or hurt, only relief. She made another small incision and sat there watching her arm slowly bleed.

The cuts were not deep enough to kill her, but now she knew she could make the final cuts, the cuts she hoped would finally put her out of her life of misery, her days of tears.

She felt a tear slide down her cheek; she hadn't noticed, but she was crying again. She closed her eyes and started to think of all the days she had cried, and remembered the days when she hadn't.

Then she felt something brush against her leg. She opened her eyes to see her cat. Her cat was eight years old, and hardly ever allowed anyone to pet her. Yet, right then, her cat was looking for affection. Her cat lay down in her lap, purring.

For the first time in months, she smiled. Instead of rubbing her knife, she started rubbing her cat. She felt something she hadn't felt in awhile—love, need, warmth. After petting her cat for half an hour, she realized she didn't want to die. She wanted her problems to go away, her friend and her to make up, but she really didn't want to die.

She will always have the small scar marks from the incisions to remind her of what happened. But she promised herself, and her cat, that she would never, ever, try or think of committing suicide again.

Nathan S. Robbins

Christine

Christine. Every time I think about grade school, my memories of Christine stand out. I went to a small Catholic grade school, a good school, for the most part. Everyone knew everyone else, and everyone was friends.

Except for Christine. She was always the outcast. The one nobody wanted. Whenever we would play a game, Christine was always last picked. Whenever we went to lunch, no one wanted to sit by Christine. And when we were supposed to have partners for a project, of course Christine didn't have a partner. So our teacher, Mrs. Sanders, would routinely call out, "OK, everybody! Christine doesn't have a partner. Who wants to be Christine's partner?"

"Yuck! Not me!"

"Ugh. I'll work alone."

"She's dirty! No one wants her!"

"Dirty girl! Dirty girl!" we all shouted.

"Stop that right now!" screamed an angry Mrs. Sanders. "Now look, Christine is crying again."

And then we would laugh some more, because we were so hilarious. After all, what could be more fun than tormenting a sixth grade girl whose hair was sometimes unkempt, and whose clothes didn't always match?

Mrs. Sanders didn't really care. We all knew she was just upset because now she had to go console the crying Christine. This kind of thing went on almost every day.

I think inside we all knew the way we treated Christine was wrong. But being friends with Christine was unthinkable. I mean, there aren't many sixth graders who can give up all their friends to be nice to the outcast. It's so hard to be an individual in sixth grade, because everything depends on what everyone else thinks of you. So Christine's torture went on, because none of us had the guts to stand up for her.

Finally, around eighth grade, people started to leave Christine alone. No one wanted to be her friend, but now they mercifully ignored her. Time passed, and Christine became quiet, shy, and almost invisible.

Later on, I learned that Christine didn't have exactly the best home life. Her life couldn't have been easy, between her home and the way we treated her. I know that the way my classmates and I acted probably affected her very deeply. To this day, she still has some of the same problems, like not having very many friends.

But it doesn't seem to matter to Christine how people treat her anymore. She smiles and laughs, even when people are terrible to her. Lately, I have been talking more to her and getting to know her.

I don't know if the rest of my class ever really changed since then. I still see them, and they are almost exactly the same. They still choose a person they consider to be not as good as them, and they take out their fears and frustrations on them, almost like a whipping boy.

I truly believe, though, that I have matured from all this. Now I try to see some good and love in all people. I know I am not the perfect person, but I am learning to be an individual. After all, I'm not in the sixth grade anymore.

Notes on Contributors

Alyssa, 16, runs track and field, and swims. Her best friends and her family are the most important things to her.

Elisabeth Andrews, 16, loves music and writing. She has received many Governor's Awards for essays and two state awards for playing the cello. Her most prized possession is her voice and she hopes to use it to touch people's lives.

Crisula Arapios, 15, enjoys being with her family and friends. Her favorite subjects are English and History.

Latoya Baker, 16, is interested in poetry.

Tony Barnhart, 17, likes to play with car stereos. His family and good friends are important to him, and he has goals.

Big Man is a student at Wayne High School who likes to collect music C.D's. He has 204.

Cravana Brew, 16, goes to Heritage High School.

Chelsea Cella is a student at North Side High School.

Shantell Corell is involved in dance, choir, cheerleading, swimming and tennis. She writes for the school paper and yearbook at North Side High School.

Janita Crandall, 17, is a student at Wayne High School. The most important thing in her life is her 18-month-old son.

Porscha Davis is a student at Heritage High School.

Adam Christopher Dennis, 17, plays hockey and baseball.

Kevin Ford, 16, likes all sports. Baseball is his favorite.

Rhett Ford, 16, likes to play baseball and basketball.

Lucas Foster is an outdoors person. He plays football and wrestles for Heritage High School.

Jared Frieden enjoys playing soccer and doing things with his friends.

Dustin Fremion, 16, loves sports, especially baseball.

Edna Ruth Hepworth is an honor student and is in Air Force ROTC. She loves to sing, dance, and just be a teenager.

Shacara Cortese Henley, 18, loves playing basketball.

Danielle Hilworth, 17, is a student at North Side High School. Her hobby is working on cars.

Rachel Jackson, 16, plays basketball. She loves children.

Kevin Jones is a student at Wayne High School.

Brandon Jordan, 18, likes playing football and hanging with his family and friends.

Justin J. Jordan, 17, is the senior class president at South Side high School. He plans to attend a four-year university. Jesus Christ is the most important thing in his life.

Matt Kissinger, 18, is interested in living life to the fullest.

Robin Lee, 16, goes to Heritage High School, where she is on the softball team. Her hobbies are swimming and shopping and her goal is to become a nurse.

Brea Lesley, 16, is interested in writing, reading poetry, and being with friends. She hopes her story will help other teens.

Terry B. Leigh, 17, is interested in sports, fishing, and watching TV. In his spare time, he collects anything that may be worth money (stamps, cards, coins).

Tod Martin is 15 and wants to see the world.

Melissa, 16, is in band, choir, FFA, volleyball, track, youth group and student council. She is the wrestling manager, and she takes piano lessons.

Freddie Owens likes to play sports.

Michelle J. Penn, 16, enjoys spending time with her family. She feels that life is a special gift that should not be taken for granted.

Steven M. Ramsey is a student at Homestead High School.

Eric Reader is a student at South Side High School.

Nathan S. Robbins, 15, enjoys singing, acting, writing, and drawing. He is in show choir, and he enjoys being with his friends.

Jennifer Schimmoller, 16, is interested in music and reading. She plans on going into the medical field.

Dusti Siefer likes to read and write poetry. She plays the viola in orchestra, sings in show choir and jazz choir, and dances (ballet, jazz, tap, and street). She dreams of having a daughter named Cecelia Grace and singing "Amazing Grace" to her every night.

Theoplis Smith, 16, is taking culinary arts and wants to live life to the fullest.

Kyla Thompson, 15, enjoys writing, singing, dancing, and acting. She loves watching football and basketball. She writes, " I hope that anyone who reads this book learns that violence doesn't help in any situation, and that there is more to life than hurting yourself or someone else."

Due to a printing error, the last three names were omitted from the list of contributors. We apologize, and give the notes on these three writers here:

Wayne Venik, 17, is a National Honor Society student who is interested in sports, music, and computers.

Carmen Warner, 16, loves art and any kind of dancing.

Jessica Willoughby, 16, plays soccer and softball for Homestead High School. She enjoys skiing, being outside, and making people laugh.

Helen Frost, editor of *Why Darkness Seems So Light,* is the author of the poetry collection *Skin of a Fish, Bones of a Bird,* the editor of the anthology *Season of Dead Water,* and the author of several books for children. Her poetry has been published in numerous journals and magazines. She has been teaching writing to children in schools, group homes, juvenile detention centers, and summer programs for more than twenty years. She is the co-author of a play based on the stories in this book.